THE MOON OVER MY MOTHER'S HOUSE

poems by

Laurie Kuntz

Finishing Line Press
Georgetown, Kentucky

THE MOON OVER MY MOTHER'S HOUSE

Publisher: Leah Huete de Maines

Editor: Christen Kincaid

Cover Art: Angie Rengifo

Author Photo: Steven DeBonis

Cover Design: Elizabeth Maines McCleavy

Order online: www.finishinglinepress.com
also available on amazon.com

Author inquiries and mail orders:
Finishing Line Press
P. O. Box 1626
Georgetown, Kentucky 40324
U. S. A.

Table of Contents

I

II

III

I

There is nothing you can see that is not a flower;
there is nothing you can think that is not the moon.

Matsuo Bashō

Infinite Tenderness

You called lost and broken down
one December night—
on a road amidst scarecrows and corn,

your car had dropped a fan belt
and I was tasked an endeavor into darkness
to find you.

The night choked me with weather and empty country roads—
no street names, nor landmarks,
just fields, leftover snow and taunting black ice.

A stranger brought you to safety that night
as darkness goaded me away from you.
Every winter storm since recalls your rage.

Once, in vengeance, I revealed
that Anna Karenina jumps in front of a train,
ruining the ending you were just about to read.

It was an ending you saw that night,
waiting for me to rescue you
from fan belts and wind.

Like Anna, I'm not good at saving others, or myself.
I fail at heroics—I'm better at baking a cake,
basting a turkey, or planting pansies—

If only I could steal myself
out from your anger,
rise to an occasion,

save you from a precipitous fall off a cliff
or venture to find your voice lost
in the Siberian wind.

Anna Karenina had infinite tenderness
but no one to save her,
unlike all the kindness that remains to rescue us.

The time we've had together leaves me breathless, as if running for a train
that I know will stop in places I never want to be again
but I board it anyway and take a window seat.

For Steven

The Moon Over My Mother's House

could never be seen,
what I remember are clotheslines
and antennas and forgotten apple trees,
fruit rotting from above
then falling to unweeded soil.
Had she wanted to see the moon
would she have known where to look?
Her life being sworn to the ground,
cemented to the day-to-day pulling
clothes off a line, quickly,
because of unexpected rain.

Lessons on Electricity, or When in Quarantine with a Husband

Who is culpable?
All the lights left burning
when we are no longer
in the rooms we share
together or alone.
Who left it on?
No cat or dog to blame,
and the son has long gone
to his own lighted place.

When admonished for this faux pas
I don't need the lecture
on wattage and currents and voltage
or the waste of power,
all I need to hear are three words,
Lights off please
or maybe those other three words
we should be saying more often
in our lighted and darkened places.

What's Sent Our Way

"How does one endure, survive, adapt, accept with grace what's sent our way?"
—Poet Lynda Hull, in a letter written to her student, S.A.

We must *endure*—
We rise each morning to the same sounds.
Birds among motors keeping us moving forward.
At times just noise, but now a welcome reminder—we are still here.

We must *survive:*
It was never easy to maneuver through all the tricks and facades
learned through the years—they all worked, up until now.

We must *adapt:*
In our evolving lexicon a new C word, more horrifying than the other,
Corona—it can be beautiful:
A pearly glow surrounding the darkened disk of the moon
Yet, every beautiful thing decays, even gilded points of a crown wear thin..

We must *accept:*
Everywhere an absence, only to see
the cloaks of the orange and black monarchs
their black wing-tipped eyes,
staring down at the amazed empty spaces,
of buildings and bike racks, and the silence of blazing bus horns.

And then there's *grace:*
This the hardest part—to relinquish power, and with sweeping wings,
fall to land into the hurdle, then attempt to rise in the face
of *what's sent our way.*

Partaking

This season's expectations
oblige the table
filled with grains and greens
and the company seated around.

To be grateful is also to learn
to forget the wrongs of the day,
the nefarious clouds,
the background noise
and all that falls away.

Some are given a chance
to move on, to be able,
to embrace a time
of silence and solitude.

Look at the sky,
catch the random flight of a hummingbird,
accept each cloud passing
over sun and land.

Our eyes,
having seen much,
beckon us back to the table to partake
despite all that has been taken away.

For Dr. CJA

To Do—When in Quarantine

Composed is a list
of the important tasks,
what one should be doing these days
but no one knows how many of these days
we have left…

So why organize the underwear drawer?
Why fill the car with antifreeze?
Is it necessary to venture into the dark
dank resources and clean every closet?
Can't those cobwebs above the drapes
pass for decoration?

Maybe *To Do* in these mercurial days
means to sit next to the cat, her purr a mantra,
find that dog-eared book and continue the reading,
really listen to the katydids in the absence of traffic,
and fill the vase with something in bloom.

If I am not here tomorrow
when they clean out my closets
who's going to care if I've
color coordinated my blouses
now hanging in empty spaces?

Hands

A man once told me I had beautiful hands,
I look at them now and try to imagine
what he saw that year I turned twenty
and gave in to his attentions
without giving anything up.

Staring hard into the past's blinded eye
are airy hands, smooth skin, slim wrists,
a time when I thought I could hold the world
and get away with it.

Since then, these hands
chapped and lined from seasons' wrath
have gnarled mercy into regret—
memories will never be as telling as moments
alone with a forbidden man.

Time will never seem so wicked
as that year a man took me into his unfurnished room,
asked nothing but to let my hands save
him from what he yearned for,

while outside the four-pane window
linden trees were in early bloom
and afterwards everything I fingered
was awe-pink, like skin across an open palm
able to hold the untouchable.

My Mother's Hands on Mother's Day

Her hands do little to nothing,
hands that once held four infants,
hemmed skirts, stirred sauces, brushed knots to silk,
hands that slapped against her life less lived,
and pulled a grandchild out of womb,
then held him up in awe—

an offering, a touch, to be of use.

Now her hands lie
idle, skin stretched and streaked
as a veined pansy petal—
Having nothing to offer,
her hands, from an empty lap,
no longer reach.

This Sunday, at the nursing home
whose walls are painted kindergarten blue,
I will hold her hands in mine,
and feel them flutter
like a butterfly caught in the wind.

For Robyne

"You weren't down for forever and it's fine"

J.P. Saxe & Julia Michaels

And here we still are,
our forevers almost done,
every moment threadbare,
full of injuries, our backs, our necks, our hips and hops,
our lives in a perpetual state of healing...
This is what forever is,
not being down for all the hurt,
the disappointments we endure
not always of our choosing
because forever is really
just loving the now.

Apples and Oranges

In February of 2020, my friend decided to join the world and get an iPhone. It was a walkable, wintery day in Arlington, and all scarved up, we walked to the neighborhood Apple store. In the store, the Geniuses were 19 years old, from the future, and sounded as if they had just completed studies at Oxford. They had sculptured profiles in various colors and politically correct tattoos adorned their sleek 24/7 yoga bodies. One of these perfect beings, our potential savior, approached and explained all things phone-like, including the meaning of life. She spoke in the infinitive case, none of her verbs ended in "ing." Kind and gentle, she tried so hard not to be condescending. She treated us like we were someone's Bubby, but not hers. In her reality, we were from another time, place and planet. I pulled out my oversized Android phone and got horrified stares from the other Apple clothed clones—- as if I were wearing a MAGA cap at a Bernie rally. After an endless morning of "silly" questions about everything "iPhoneish," my friend had her new pink iPhone. We walked out of the store with years of guarantees, a new language to master, and links to virtual this and that's. I wanted to yell back to every person in that store that I went to Woodstock, that I was cool before they were a gleam in anyone's plans. But, I didn't, I was only to be remembered as that Android lady from another planet. This all took place on February 22, 2020. Today, as we are in the *cruelest months,* we all find ourselves on the same planet, all speaking the same language.

For Joix and Carol

Meraki

A Greek word meaning to do something with soul, creativity and love,
leaving a piece of yourself in what has been created.

"I Looked at the Turtle And the Turtle Looked Back at Me"
is something one would say to a child,
but I said this to my son, turning 29,
after I came back from the pond where
ibis and egrets waded, and it was there
almost on the water's edge, I eyed a turtle
and it eyed me, and at that moment I remembered
the lore of a grand turtle rising up from the deeps
with mud on its shell, the first soil of the world
heaped on its back to create the Earth.
My son, with a broken foot, could not venture
to the pond that day, leaving me alone with
a turtle bearing the weight of the world on its shell
but he promised, when all was healed, to come to the rim
of the pond and look for the turtle who looked at me,
carrying a piece of itself upon shores of love.

Morocco in a Moment

Wet cobblestones and tight alleyways
lead to a calico cat sprawled
against a blue wood door, slightly ajar,
exposing the veiled lady in the shadowed frame.

Our shared dark eyes meet.
No language, but gestured commonalities.
I bend toward her cat rubbing against my ankles.
Perfect purrs accept a stranger's hand.

This woman and I share a smile
but only for a moment—then we return
to our strange, strange, separate lives.

Asuncion

Details which once belonged to us
slip off memory's hanger like a silk shirt—

the famous battle,
that actor who always plays the villain
or is it the hero—a jazz refrain,
beloveds' birthdays,
and the names of well navigated cities
are lost in the tattered purse of recollection
like the capital of Paraguay.

Not that the capital of Paraguay means much to many
but we were there, you and I, in November
when mangoes fell from trees lining the boulevard.

We stuffed our packs and pockets full
and ate them under moonlight
when no one was looking
and the world was mango-wonderful.

Now, I do forget—

to buy your favorite cereal…
to turn lights off…to tie the dog up…
forget that I annoy.

But I do remember the capital of Paraguay.

We were there once, you and I,
knapsacks cabooosed to our backs,
bellies filled with fallen mangoes—

Living for days on just that fruit.

Not Drowning But Waving

A spin off Stevie Smith's *Not Waving But Drowning*

I was out too far, too deep,
instead of fearing the undertow
I floated, followed my heart's compass
and found myself in a place
where the tide gently spoke to the shore—

this is what hope is truly about,
the bird with feathers
that swoops in grace
and finds its appetite sated in sea salt.

I swim out for a closer look
at that pelican now perched
on a buoy, which is stamped
with the message:

Do not anchor here

I don't—I keep swimming
far, but close enough
to where you can see
I am not drowning, but waving.

Epiphany for the Husband

It was a weird dream:
I was in a coma
but I woke
and you were there
by my bedside
your gratitude shining.

My first words were:

I have been mean to you for so many years

and you said: *That's your epiphany?*

Well, you have to be mean to someone
and you don't want to be mean to the dog
and the cat will be doubly mean right back at you.

Palooka

Downstairs battling midday heat
I hear end of round bells coming
from the TV room overlooking the view
our house offers of ocean and blue horizons.

Father and son, now men,
aging and old, mesmerized,
not by the sea, tern trills
or sailing vessels embracing
silence and wind, but by chants
for left hooks, sucker punches,
parrying, pluck and sweat—

how they sit in peace
and bond over cheers for blood
and the pummeling of men.

II

There is no greater agony than bearing an untold story inside you.
Maya Angelou

Mother Haibun

The haibun form is traditionally used for recording a location in a concentrated prose block, and ends with a 'whisper' of sorts to the reader in the form of a haiku

The rain reminds me of days when I would wait for the taxi to take me to the home
full of nurses and orderlies and slow elevators slinking up to the 6th floor.
The quiet floor, with a lonely view of sky, sea and rain clouds,
which followed me on every visit. I sat with my mother in silence,
tracking the lines on her face, visualizing my future,
her countenance, a crooked smile.
I wiped away the drool, which ran down her chin like rain drops—
a smear on the glass pane that I stared out of.
I never wanted to remember her like this, as she dozed with labored breath,
but I do, recalling an August sea churn going from:

Clear blue
to a tarnished mix
of wave and storm.

The Weight of Silence

The night is noisy,
not with motors
but with a thunderclap
of frog croaks and a rude wind—
if I turn a corner, the surf sounds,
if I leave my solitude
motors, motors everywhere,
even past the dusky light.

One night, I brought my son to the veranda
and asked him, between the bark of dogs
and the clash of katydids and crickets
where is pure silence—
the sound of no sound?

He turned the moment
to physics, vacuums, and deep space
but my thoughts could not hold his instructive voice,
wanting so much to escape the noise of facts,
until he said what I could understand:

When we stand in quietude
eventually, a heart beat will be heard.

Away From Her

I want to remember my mother when she was still herself,
not in a grip of sorrows and congestions.
As death sits at her table, I am away from her
now, the last questions can never be answered,
no going back to mother and daughter
only on to the dealings with death.

Cummings said, *Dying is fine*

but my mother is hooked up to a life gone stagnant,
there is only the waiting, but once gone
and out of the aching descent,
I will easily remember a woman
holding in her palms the lines
of all her children's futures.

As death eats at her table, I am away from her
picking huckleberries from trees rooted in my daily paths—
like a child I engage in pulling down the heavy berried limbs
carrying such sweetness, the way a mother carries
the wishes and woes of her children.

When I should be near, I am far
picking huckleberries, their juices run
over my crescent finger tips and stain my skin—

stains that remain for days
like the memory of my mother
when she was still herself.

For Marc, Jay, and Robyne

Self Portrait

That's me, the stick figure caught
in a cobweb.

My sparrow limbs can easily slide
out through the fragile filament

but my fingers, caught in sticky strands,
refuse to unclench

and create this intricate tangle
of crisscross gossamer.

I am both
the spindled figure caught

and the weaver who spins a lacey spider silk,
unable to escape, and yet at ease

in a lattice of trapping designs.

For the Broken

I threw an apple core skyward
to see if it would reach the moon.

It fell into a field of wild roses
which were eventually cut and posed
in a vase centered on a table
set with blue dragon cups.

Apple cores, cut flowers, porcelain tea cups:
a conscious choice between wonder and wonderful.

When poetry no longer mends
what has so long been broken
unsullied moonlight shining on a field of roses
replaces words—

stanzas tossed skyward
singe roses clean of thorns.

For Minh Sen

Survivors: After Stories of Many

The sky splinters in slivers of violet
this last day of July collared
in Queen Anne's Lace and bracelets of clover.
You regret the lilac bush outside our father's house
has had an early bloom.

As children, we'd pick the fallen clusters
off the ground, press them
in his heavy books, then forget.
Years later, when I turned a page
a resemblance of lilac fell
on the blanket covering him.

At the funeral, you murmur,
I'm only here because he's dead.
And once again, the creak
and stir of your bedroom door wakes me.

All those years, I wanted to scream for you,
for both of us, but what good
would it have done?

I couldn't imagine what could save me
from his open, hissed kiss,
that chapped palm against my lean body.
I never warned you of his approaching step
always echoing heavily through feigned dreams.

We don't speak of this or the dead
but walk from the gravesite
among all we can name,
milkweed, tiger lily, bloodroot

the path overgrown since childhood
when we played with wild snapdragons,
your hand pressed over mine,
just the right pressure, where to pinch

and the yellow tongued flower
parted its lips.

Ghost Shoes

My mother dozes
while I gather her collection
of hoarded shoes.

The white noise
of a game show, *Deal or No Deal*
stirs my mother—everything becomes muted
by coughs and raspy requests
for pills and pillows.

I suggest Goodwill
for the old heels with buckles
that only the nimblest of fingers
can do or undo.

She wags an arthritic finger and says:
The woes of the dead are inherited in ghost shoes.
My glare scolds her belief in old wives' tales.

Yet she sees, in between wake and dreams,
all the old wives coming to visit:
Gilda, Faye, and Pearl wearing sling backs,
asking her to walk along the avenue.

How easily they beckon
from her bedside or TV screen,
the only view she now has.

Before the next reverie
or the emcee's call
of a once in a lifetime bargain,
I gather all the shoes,
the gilded bows and rhinestone straps,
the thin heels she could once balance upon.

When realizing their fated donation,
she grabs the black heels with the red bow

and states in a voice conjured for a last request:
                    Keep these
I can see her strolling steadily
with the wives that come for her,
and the white noise of the game show
becomes my own voice, shouting
like noisy audience revelers: *Deal !*

The Wind Speaks

After the poem *Wind* by James Arthur

It's true, sometimes I cannot stop myself
and something sweet, like sugared coffee
set on a summer porch, spills.

A door slams before anyone is allowed
into a warm yellowing room.

The cap that protects from the rage of noon
flaps in a kite dance.

But then again, I am there to make chimes spin,
spread a crimson sheet of cherry blossoms over grey streets
and settle powdered snow banks against a decaying brick wall.

And you, I can change your moods and cool an anger,
make you hear the song of stones
sweeping red earth away.

You can see a clearing
in the horizon, get a different view
as I slap you in an embrace...
                            And carry blood to your cheeks.

Wabi Sabi

Japanese aesthetic: An appreciation for what is broken or thread bare or unfinished.

My life is unfinished,
I sit by a window, where
puddles fill with repetition,
and struggle to end a day
not with the same stare tasking sadness,
but with vision of some new thing.

Red leaves settle under the dying tree.
I stop thinking and winnow out the motors
hear a cricket spill its night call
with no end in sight to the evening's voice.

There is retreat and shade,
the alley cat knows to seek
the same spot underneath a dwelling—

In the sea of my broken life,
lies a threadbare promise.

In the Absence of Healing

After the cold and fever
an intermittent hacking
cough comes to remind
things are not quite healed.

What ails, the bristling wind, the distant
explosion, fault lines tilting.
The expectations are to pen every tragic moment
into a healing metaphor.

I think of flowers
but my son, at 26, his life in bloom,
tells me to stop writing about flowers,
yet all my disasters find rhyme

with larkspur and Queen Anne's lace,
and in the absence of healing,
I think of tulips, frozen and waiting
under February's wrath.

Salubrious

Salūbris: invigorating health—

That was my father's favorite word
but I did not know this
until my brother, delivering his eulogy,
faltered over the story
how my father, in the throes
of dementia, would ask:

Are you salubrious today?

hoping his children's answers
would whet a memory
astray in the warrens of his mind,
lost in time's dark tunnels.

As I stare into my son's face
beneath a salubrious sky,
the wish remains,

that nothing will be forgotten.

For Marc

Wonder and Words:

Thinking of Ferlinghetti on His 100th Year

Just to live to be 100,
one would think is enough
or too much.

To be a poet
at 100, to see the world in daily
verse, in metered awe, every
day an enjambment, spilling

years of words into understanding
what saves us
from lies, and bad
governments, and all the hype.

An end-stop, making us pause
and ponder the words of an old man
who, still, can take a daily walk,
hear the squawk of crows

and notice the yellow primrose peeking
through cement—
an old man who still believes
poetry can heal, and lives year after year,
convincing us with words.

"A Heart Needs a Home"

a line in a song by Richard Thompson

An excess of heart,
that is what you said about the poem
I wrote for you.

Take the "heart" out, simply stated,
find another image for the beat of our lives:

two decades ago, a doctor pulled out a syringe
to draw from our son's veins—testing
to make sure he was not a carrier of some drastic disease.

When, Noah, barely two, saw that needle,
he yelled, *Blood,* one of his first words,

we did not know where he had learned this
but our son knew *blood* by heart,

that blood tying us to our shared strangeness and similarities,
blood leading to heart lines—

taking the *heart* out,
is like forgetting about the cunning rain
on days when all is in bloom.

Driving Back to El Monte

In your first winter, before El Nino,
when the weather was still predictable
and there was part-time shift work,
Bich gardened and the yard seeded into a lush profit
of fuchsia, bluebells, and guava trees.

Crimson morning glory bolted up a wooden trellis
and in a stone pool under the mossy cover
of lotus pods, Japanese Koi shimmered
like gold bricks that paid your way to California.

Draping wisteria
shaded Bich's bedroom window
and the scent of guava woke her
most mornings, as it had in Vietnam.

The rent was controlled,
the garden wasn't, set apart from the eyesores
along Elliot Ave, and you both lived under the bloom
of all that had been scattered.

Then, the owners, needing a place
for their arriving Ensenada relatives,
gave you a month's notice and you moved closer
to the minimum wage and better bus routes.

And that's how it was

until one day, wanting for something to lament,
you drove Bich back down Elliot Avenue,
both of you waiting for that splash of color.

What is it that makes people want
to cut everything down to blacktop,
or the need for something concrete?
You parked, blocking the driveway
and named the flowers gone,
the trees severed to stumps,

and the weeds warily waved like lovers
departing from distant docks.

For the Pham family

Khartoum to Karachi

that was her destination
leaning toward the final flight
on the sliver of silver
the remainder of dreams—
crashing in the desert,
the fear of not doing so,
then the landing in Calcutta,
factories and rickshaws, train whistles,
the contemplation of civilization
where, unlike the sky, lie beginnings and endings.
But this is not about Amelia
or her navigation through everyone's
egg- blue frontier, this is about truce
and the bare distance between continents and a hug
as blue deepens, boundaries cross and speech
translates to the language of the sky,
where capture and rescue are one and the same.

Packing to Travel: My Son's College Graduation

Your father asks me:
do I want to take a flashlight?
His practical packing annoys
yet his simple question
sheds history on who he is
and why I am still here.

I look to take trinkets
and protect them in a wrap of sock balls.
This time, I found your baby bracelet
Baby Boy,
You went unnamed for seven days
until we were sure all 2 pounds and 12 ounces
of you would grace our lives.

Again, he asks: What about the flashlight?
I snap a quote from Kubrick, your favorite,

However vast the darkness, we must supply
our own light.

And add:
I 'm packing light,
laughing at the pun.
But the radiated reality
is that I'd ask you the same
and if met with protest,
into your luggage,
I would sneak the light
then hand you extra batteries.

Not Flowers

There are still
times in our lives together
that I listen for the car engine
to roll into the dirt driveway,
feel like a young girl
excited to meet your gaze,
and help you unwrap parcels of your day.

It was like that today,
a first Friday of sun and little wind
and when you walked in, carrying
bunches of green stems wrapped
in old newsprint, they looked, from this distance,
like gladiolas, and in a vision I dusted off
a celadon vase.

But when I approached you
already in the kitchen,
I saw the peaks of long green onions
being unwrapped from yellowed newspaper,

and in silence, I picked up a knife
and began to chop.

Nihongo Whispers

After the diaries of Kawai Koume 1804-1889 and Ishikawa Takuboku
1886-1912

Yoshiko, 1849

These are not easy times for a Samurai's wife,
the streets fill with strange men,
children throw stones
and the river has become unsafe for merchants—
no fresh catch for days,

last night Shokuko's husband was slashed
from the forehead down—
these details, come from other samurai
who, in times of peace,
compose *hokku*..

Gazing at blossoms
butterflies pass, tired wings
seek muted flowers

Kiyo, 1853

A glass bead bracelet, from *itoko*,
living across oceans, arrived for me.
If I look inside each ball
I see a woman's face,
her coarse features frighten,
so unlike the Edo goddess who,
naked from the sky over Nagoya,
danced over rice fields.

These nights amidst festival lanterns
people take the hands of strangers and samurai,
joined and singing, *Yoi ja nai ka, yoi ja nai ka,*
Ohari pours from the sky,

from cock's crow to the sun's fall.
Many days, now things have tumbled from clouds,
sliver, copper, rice and talismans,
the streets full of persimmons and tangerines.

On the third day over voices
of *yoi ja nai ka*, the shogun resigns,
the cries diminish.

Murasaki, The Satsuma rebellion, 1877

Newspapers for sale, two sen,
how cheap to read of lives gone at Kumamoto,
who shall win?

The rebels, demons,
if they had ten crowns
it would be too few to cut off.

The heads of troop commanders
have been sent back
pickled in salt, name tags on their ears.

Villagers volunteer, men over 17 and under 40
go, today, when the weather is fine
and the peonies are opening.

Umeko, 1879

Men who have walked in secrecy
call for me, after their battles.
I sing and dance, bathe them in the mineral waters,

perhaps they have wives rivers away,
sleeping under quilts, fine ivory hands
restless across the thick quilted *futons.*

Nihongo Whispers Revisited

It was on a walk, a thing we do together
with the dog, in the woods, by our house.
You told me you came across an old poem of mine,
 your favorite, based on found diaries
of Japanese women—the whispers of their lives
during war, during spring, during love that gets lost.

I wanted to tell you that I wrote that poem during
a time when our love was lost—in the spring,
love in need of dusting off the lint of winter woes.
But I said nothing, just smiled,
and quoted a line or two from that poem—
all I could remember.

Today, I start this new poem, again
our love is lost, again in spring.
Is it because here in the north
April often wears February's wrath?
While I write, in the background, wind and vacuum,
another woman cleans my house, and I listen,
and think of those drawers I cannot bear to open.

By Invitation Only

Just when you think you can hear beyond
the mowers and raw hum of traffic
to the sounding in high tree tops of the hermit thrush,
when you think the bougainvillea's shades have deepened overnight
to wine hues, and the scent of oleander smacks
the sultry hour with its powdered perfume,
and just as you feel you are ready to accept
a purse full of disappointments
and the sinews inside your heart
have separated song from static,
finally humming an invitation to happiness,
just when the world is quiet, and you can entertain loss
like an invited guest who asks to sip
from whatever you are drinking
but instead spills something deeper
that seems to pour from the nub of sadness—
and just when you think you must continue to entertain this discontent,
you let it drip onto the bouquet of lilies you have just picked from a garden
that insists on blooming in spite of what has just happened.

III

Memory is one of my strongest muses
Marge Piercy

Caring for Erica in April

Diamonds and daisies,
Venus, the morning star,
the evening star,
Aperire, an opening—
a time when all things resurrect
from their own personal winters.

That is when I arrived
to braid her hair,
keep the tangles at bay,
a fine, silken reminder
much like the cats that covered her
as she lay in bed, whispering
each name: Zeke, Coal, Sebastian, Tabby,
and told stories of their rescue.

I was not there to rescue,
only to watch old movies,
talk about distant lands,
past lovers, and the trees
she could see outside her window
but could no longer care for.

Sometimes, on those opening spring mornings,
I would rake a patch of weeds, and her cat, Zeke,
would bring gifts from his nightly hunt
and place them under the kumquat tree
laden with a heavy April bloom.

For Erica and Kathryn
and all the cats

Tailgating the Ambulance

We must have been reeling,
my hand straddling your crotch,
the possession I had over you
more intoxicating than the speed limit we broke
tailgating the ambulance, so close
I could see the old woman, her hand
resting on the brow of her husband strapped to a gurney
and I wondered aloud—would we be together that long?
You faltered, in that tentative voice, the one
that still keeps you from making promises,
yet here we are sharing sciatica stories—

we stopped for a red light,
the ambulance did not.

It is only now I hear the sirens beginning to sound.

Tailgating the Ambulance, Revisited

Almost 70, you start
every argument with
we will die soon.
That *soon* happened at 1 AM,
sprawled on a bathroom floor,
eyes that once could read a recipe written in Thai,
hands that could sketch 500 kanji characters,
and a mind that could grasp spark plugs to super novas
were vacant, cold, fading—

hooked up to beeps and lines and veins replenished
in an ambulance traveling faster than light years,
I saw your head through the fog of my worried windshield
and I remembered—

we were 20,
tailgating an ambulance on the streets of Brooklyn
wondering about the couple inside,
giving them a history, which would soon be defunct—

we are them— history repeating itself.

Sky Blue

Do you remember how Noah, at six,
creating his own history,
badgered us with questions
about our favorite dessert, song, movie, color?
Exasperated and not wanting to ponder,
we made up answers—

Pudding, Blackbird, Arsenic and Lace, Indigo

These days, we forget
to ask what it is that honors us
and I worry, after all this time together,
what escapes is the infinite capacity
to recognize our true hearts

and I won't know what song to play at your funeral,
what color shirt to dress you in
or what sweets to serve the onlookers of my grief.

I start to stack up the answers by asking something simple:
your favorite color—
and you, avoiding simplicity, conjure this:

Long Bay, seen from the hill,
where sky swallows sea,
before we take the curve
leading to shore, and home.

Home to the veranda we now stand on,
beginning again, under a moon growing full,
and the sea and sky turning a deeper shade of blue.

Don't Think Twice It's All Right

Some things I will never do well:

so when you picked up your guitar
and asked me to sing,
after a slight hesitation,
unsure if the air was riddled,
I followed you into song—

Dylan being our captain—
certain that the chorus
was a metaphor for our lives,

we gave our hearts by sacrificing a bit of our souls,

but perhaps it is time to ignore the words,
relish the cadence,
the moment—
we are both carrying the tune.

Thinking of Dead Poets Among the Homeless

A rare rain in Los Angeles.
NPR a white noise on the car radio
as I stared down the homeless makeshift shelters littering
the Cahuenga Blvd Exit, and my son, an expert freeway driver,
asks:

Do you know the recently dead poet they are speaking of?

But I was not listening to the car radio,
I was thinking of rain in the desert,
homeless in the streets,
and the manicured gardens behind the tall gates.

My son kept on asking,
Don't you know this poet?

Then, I heard the commentator quote:

Let us stifle under mud at the pond's edge,
and affirm that it is fitting and delicious to lose everything.

Of course, I knew the poet,
so many dead poets,
so many homeless,
so many lawns being cared for
by those living far from the 101,
speaking in various tongues,
residing in their own makeshift poems.

Hysterical Blindness

Let's start with something beautiful.

I expect her to invoke incense burning
in brass holders, lotus ponds on temple grounds.
Or her daughter's slim shoulders covered
in printed Cambodian silk, arms swaying
to brass gongs, bamboo flutes.

But her eyes only twitch and flutter.
Late autumn light seeps
through venetian blinds,
the light she misses the most,
the sphere of light from gilded pagodas,
dawn light across her courtyard, spreading.

It's light that haunts her.
What do I know of the sharp gleam
she saw in the edge of a soldier's blade
held against her husband's throat?

Can she remember the shape of her daughter's lips?
I ask her to describe the last face she saw
or the last color she wore.

Let's start with something beautiful.

Her eyes, for a moment, focus,
her head tilts toward me—
This blindness, she says, *this blindness.*

Kintsukuroi

*To repair with gold: The Japanese art of repairing pottery with gold
or silver lacquer and understanding that the piece is more beautiful
for having been broken*

What is it about glistening glass veins
restored with gold that makes us hope
sadness, like pottery, will break?

Sharpened shards needing to be restored,
the cracked vase spills fresh cut gladiolas,
beauty we depend on is never contained.

Our porcelain hearts can no longer hold—
our child, our home, ourselves—
the cracks widen until filled with golden insight:

we are more beautiful for being broken.

Kansha Sai

That's Japanese for *Thanksgiving,*
"The festival of gratitude."
Here I am in Japan
at the end of November
alone, giving thanks.

It was a poet that said "Alone is a stone."
Today the stones are shimmering
under a fading fall sun
and to be alone allows the landscape of memory
to stir under this wizened sky.

My son was once afraid of the sky,
he never wanted to look up
thinking he would be swallowed.

Today, I am thankful
he has gotten over that fear.
Thankful for much on this day
when bombs are going off elsewhere.
But there are always bombs going off
and we carry our own inner grenades
waiting to explode into a sullen sky.

Yet, I remain grateful:
for sons, for stones that shimmer,
for an ebbing autumn,
knowing that alone, I am together
with so many who are like scattered seeds
ripening into buds and waiting to bloom
in all the places I am not.

Aftershocks

It starts slowly, a rumble
a faint tremble, the light bulb shakes,
the windows wrench, crushing glass sounds

                    the reign of distant chimes.

In the end, all things not secured tumble.

A woman from Syria
rarely goes out, and not without
a scrutinizing eye—
the safest corner.
A table away from windows.
She avoids buses, walks everywhere,
but not in that carefree swagger
barely afforded to the children who walk beside her.

My Cambodian neighbor wakes most nights
from the same dream—
mistaking the wind for thunder,
thunder for memories,
the picture of her eldest
falls off the night table.

So many years ago now
my sister drove over the Brooklyn Bridge
smelling the charred papers
that fell from the sky for days.
Excavations, foundations set,
blueprints blown against an approaching wind—
not a bone was returned to her.

In the end, all things not secured tumble
                    into a reign under distant chimes.

Where to Put the Crayons

is what my son feared
                              on his first day
in the new kindergarten class,
                    holding his own box of crayolas
with new color names:
                    burgundy, tawny flesh, crimson, teal blue,

these wonder wands twisting lines

                    into anteaters or antelopes,
                                        capes or crowns

but after the mystery of the making
                                        when he was done
where would he put his waxing hues—
                              on what reachable shelf
of his five year old heart
                    would all these colors fit?

All this magic having to be cleaned
                              up and packed away neatly
          even though someone with a sturdier hand
                              had printed his name squarely
          on the box,

a name on a box he could recognize,

                    but was still not sure
                              where it belonged.

Rescue

Miklos Radnoti, a writer from Budapest fell victim to the Holocaust. The Jewish Hungarian poet was shot in the head by German guards on forced march from Yugoslavia to Hungary during the last days of WWII In a mass grave, two years later, Radnoti's body was discovered and exhumed. His last poems, written on postcards, were found in his coat pocket.

Radnoti, a twin, rescued at birth, lived in halves,
thinking of the mother and brother who didn't survive
and how, from the wondrous womb,
he was hurled into a world where fathers, too, leave
a year before a boy becomes a man.

Left with whole lives gone,
Radnoti suffered the copper mines,
labor camps and death marches,
nothing spared but his words—

poems written to his wife
on bits of paper, backs of postcards,
cured from ground to seed against time
and the hands of men raking lands irreverent—

all unearthed, as Radnoti wrote,
"Patience flowers into death now."

Delphiniums grow from the dirt,
the discarded mass, the rancid heap
where Radnoti's body rotted,
bone on pebble, ink on gravel,
all that is rescued from soil to flower.

The Promise

I can't remember when it was made,
what we were doing,
but I felt your hand
smooth on my face
as you promised
I would always be beautiful.
And I believed you,
a man of few promises,
fearing the spoken word,
its eggshell fragility and power
to break at a clumsy touch.
I imagined I could live
not fearing time or betrayal…
until now, still grateful
you are here, but the promise broken,
as your rugged hand skims my face,
an encounter of pits and furrows,
my Braille skin, an oath
only the blind can read.

The Silk Kimono Jacket

has been tossed in this bargain box,
its sleeves tangle in waves
of faded silk swans and blooming
flower patterns, purple and peach run
from the horn of the iris's trumpet.

Many have worn it...
the wedding jacket of a milk maiden,
a gift for a mistress,
or a woman's city coat.

Balled lint lines the pelican pockets,
a crumpled tissue, a wooden button, a hairpin,
Women grew in and out of this fabric
like the billowing of sails on erratic seas.

Cranes and flowers reeled together,
a rhymed pattern of seasoned colors.
The musky silk shimmers—in my hand, a palette of lives.

The years of wear are many...
I could settle on a lower price,
but it is not the bargain I want,
just the tight weave of memories.

A Basket Set on the Shore

(Remembering the March 2011 tsunami, Japan)

An ordinary day, until it wasn't.
Go up they said, *to higher ground,*

her body was never found
disappearing from the rooftop,
the closest place to heaven.

Years later, a mother still searches,
rebuilding a life becomes routine
and daily, the ocean reminds her—

her daughter's days were far
from extraordinary, but gentle
like the tide during a crescent moon.

She makes an offering each evening—
salted plums, bean cakes, ginger tea,
placing each item in a basket,
setting it on the shore

and as mourning has no geography,
heading home, her back to the rising tide,
she does not watch as the sea eats.

The Dahlia's Lament

Alone with your dad
and his present:
a single red dahlia

which I potted in fresh soil,
and placed in a shaded far
corner of my garden.

On Mother's Day
you are 21, in Denmark
without a plan in your pocket

but to see a girl.

Your Ophelia,
my dahlia,
damn Denmark.

I am at the start
of every mother's
journey.

Starfish and Sons

Is it because of all the lunches I did not forget to make,
or the times, on those first school days, I never overslept
when you needed someone to find you under masses
of covers, and open the shades to blankets of light?
I marvel that I never forgot to get you the shots you needed
to survive childhood and its diseases
or to buy you gloves and shoes that would not slip
on slippery slopes, and to pick you up on those corners of traffic and noise,
those intersections where sons yearn to hear that familiar horn
and enter a car whose windows fog with heat and doors click,
shutting the world away, speeding home
to the wonder of starfish and sons,
who grow into their own shores,
despite what a mother did or did not forget to do.

Monarch in January

One January morning, from an unseen corner
out flew a Monarch, this queen of color,

braving in winter the flight of fragility.
While generations retreated

from ice and wind and frozen limb
this one butterfly,

tired of migrating away from cold,
against all instinct found, between frozen airways,

space for her coral wings to nest.
As she landed on my snow brushed glove,

icy star tipped flakes on limp, felt fingertips,
began to melt.

Butterflies and Sirens

(A response to the sudden migration of Painted Lady Butterflies to Los Angeles, spring of 2019)

I was there for the rain
but left

before the early bloom
of nettles and mallows,

was absent
when the angel-voiced siren of Los Angeles

taunted the Painted Ladies north
to feast on lupines and milk weed,

everywhere
the cloak of orange,

their black wing-tipped eyes,
staring down at the amazed denizens

while skimming by buildings
and bike racks and bus horns blazing.

Hundreds in mid-day light, hovering,
while the sirens of the city

blared through this place of comings and goings
drawing all to look closer

at the shock of arrival,
the surprise of flight

and a noon epiphany,
the sirens' calls—

announcing the end of the drought.

The Blue Butterfly of Fukushima

> I do not know whether I was then a man dreaming I was a butterfly, or whether I am now a butterfly, dreaming I am a man."
> —Zhuangzi, *Butterfly as Companion: Meditations on the First Three Chapters of the Chuang-Tzu*

Within a year, the blue butterfly changed,
barely noticeable,   the wingspread limited,
the markings on the underbelly a faded hue,
shorter antennae, dented eyes—

Its pale grass blue color muted, the butterfly flies,
but within boundaries, much more like man,

fading to the blue in an endless sky.

Husband Rebuilding the Engine

He does things like that.
Oiled bolts spread on a tarp.
In old military issue coveralls,
not camouflaging his own disasters
of stalls and spills,
nuts and springs clamor
onto the belly of the engine.
I want him to seek a mechanic
but he needs to conquer
this jetsam and flotsam of steel.
I come out, hold the hood up,
turn the key, push the pedal to the floor.
He listens for the hum, that perfect pitch.
He'll spend hours doing just this.
I call him for dinner,
I call him for a bath
I call him for love,
there is no time, but this time,
watching him under a single bulb
waiting for the motor to ignite,
he rebuilds all that fails him
into something that turns over and runs.

C is for Cactus

The cactus in your August garden,
there for over a decade,
blossomed its yearly magenta orb
the same time that a flower of cells
 inside your breast multiplied,

no sweet red flower
surrounded by spikes
to ward away an enemy,
but a dividing clump of cells
offering no protection.

I want you to be the cactus
that survives in arid ground—
you, who have always loved the desert,
its stark soil and ruby suns,
now must cope with your own terrain.

The cactus flower will dry and drop,

leaving tawny spines to protrude
on its flat green armor
defending what is lost.
It remains beautiful in the land it is rooted in.

For MMN, AS, and DK

Invisible

Catcalls
now are real screeches
I hear, at midnight, from my bed facing an alley.

No one wants to help me change a tire.

The black, low cut dress does not work, nor even fit.

Yet I dance
with feet alight,
though no one watches.

In torn, stained tees, I walk without fear

of anyone following, or calling, or grabbing.
I can curse aloud,
no one hears, when I say:

I am here,
I have proof—
lines, scars, the stretchy skin

I still live in.

Icarus Flying

Before the fall, Icarus flew—

Every bird, curious and jealous
of his unabashed wingspread,
and how he, unjaded as a starling,
approached, on the verge of victory,
the open, forgiving blue tear
between the nefarious clouds.

With austere abandon, we seek,
in what we love, the same victory—

Hoping our wings will withstand,
but in the end, it is not the strength
of feathers and wax, or splendor of flight—

What astonishes is knowing
at the journey's end, how to land.

Icarus at 30

Had he lived, what would he be like?
What self imposed labyrinths
would he have to escape?
What if waxy wings and wispy feathers held true
or had he listened more closely, not been taken
by the freedom that befell him in a moment of bliss,
all the advice he could have heeded,
the many days he would have loved,
but he succumbed to the splendor of wings
before he knew that life could be contained in places
where flight is a choice, rather than a necessity
as the universe gives us so many winged creatures,
and then us, who have feet on fortunate ground.

For my son on his 30th year

Hamlet, Happy at 31

Let's assume, the King is still alive
and Gertrude not the whore her son believes her to be.
Ophelia learns to swim, and the flowers she picks
for her garland bloom in a myriad of bright shades,
casting no shadow, no need for Hamlet
to wear a sharp crown of revenge.

Let's assume no one is stalking the borders of madness
and swords' tips become dull for lack of necessary use
for the kingdom knows peace as Hamlet, turning 31,
his palette of woes dry, may still at times see ghosts,
but they never speak of betrayal
as the prince prepares for a glittering, well-deserved crown.

For my son on his 31st yea

Peonies and Peacocks

After a painting by Maruyama Okyo (1733-95)
painted in 1777 during the Edo Period

In Japan, spring peonies bloom and girls learn
of the subtle opening of petals,
the faint odor of a blossoming season.
Mothers whisper, *tateba shakuyaku*, behave like a peony,
grace in fullness, reserve in a showy petal.

Maruyama paints peonies as backdrop,
fading flowers become ground cover
under peacocks strutting their palettes
and muting all other colors.

To look beyond the painting
is to enter a garden at dusk
and see tulips closing as the cicadas' drone
harmonizes with the conversation of women
who wear the luxury of rose scented baths.

Their kimonos swish in the grace of windswept grass,
they finger blue and white teacups,
dwell on the fine sip of conversation,
and by the peonies' blind bloom they stand on ceremony
accepting the dimming light, the truth about petals,
and the conceit of the strutting peacock
living in grace and ceremony
not far beyond the scope of the picture.

Poem to My Unborn Grandchild in Covid-19 Times

When I think *future,*
it's a wisp of thought on the wing
of the lone monarch hovering
and unleashing an imagined tomorrow
around the milkweed.

What will you see of this world?

Today in the quiet of distance
the world blooms against the trill
of a yellow-rumped warbler and cicadas at dusk.
The dormant bougainvillea surprises me
with a purple thrush of crested petals.

How will this world crown you?

A child arriving in these times,
learning to embrace the future
in tiny conceived moments.

Putting Weight on the Earth

Just before your 71st year
you fell, close to home,
from a borrowed bike.

After days of cold waiting rooms
and x-rays, you were given the right
to put weight on all that hurts.

When I voice texted this to those concerned,
it played: *He is allowed to put weight on the Earth.*

In this time of auto correctness,
every word spins to a perfect ending.
Yet we are here not to be perfect,
or correct in all we do.

Sometimes we fall,
from what is borrowed, like time,
but we can find ourselves getting up, once again,
when we are given permission
to put weight on the Earth and all that hurts.

Epiphany for the Husband

It was a weird dream:
I was in a coma
but I woke
and you were there
by my bedside,
your gratitude shining.

My first words were:

I have been mean to you for so many years

and you said: *That's your epiphany?*

Well, you have to be mean to someone,
and you don't want to be mean to the dog,
and the cat will be doubly mean right back at you.

Poem For a Man Who Whistled

It was not your breath,
chilled and dry, filling the room,
that woke me all those mornings
but that whistle, something tuneless,
as you undressed, entered my bed
and covered your face with my hair
still tangled in dreams.

This year the linden tree
has had an early bloom,
marking the end of a winter spent alone.
If you were to come back to this room
you would find it the same,
things untouched, as in a still life.

Sometimes, before undressing,
I catch myself whistling
something tuneless,
nothing I can put words to.

At the Vietnam Memorial

In July, there's always a crowd
passing in single file,
muttering names of those they know,
each memory distinct in marble.

I look for Billy O'Conner,
the shy boy from Hubbard Place,
his immortality earned through a failing
grade in Geometry.

And Tony Russo, who said
he'd rather work the vineyards of Italy
than go to Nam, but he went, stained
with my best friend's virginity.

As names on black marble slope to grass,
people disperse and rush to parked cars
before the meter raises its flag.

I walk toward the hills
a hazy sun moves to dusk,
casting elongated shadows.

From where I stand
not a single name can be seen,
only the reflection of the living.

Me Too, Me Three, Me Many

How terribly strange to be abused
by an uncle,
a father,
a neighbor,
a teacher,
a doctor.
Remaining silent at 17,
not tell anyone
for fear.
You are at fault.
You are to blame.
You are wrong.
You are less than
your father,
your neighbor,
your teacher,
your doctor.
How terribly strange to know
your friend was abused
by an uncle,
a father,
a neighbor,
a teacher,
a doctor
remaining silent at 18,
at 33, at 54, at 65.
Not tell anyone
for fear.
She is at fault, She is wrong,
even together, you feel less
than all the power men amass.
Reveal their lies,
and feast on comfort
in someone's story.
How terribly strange to have a dark secret,
but somewhere in the telling
you live, she lives.

Me two, Me three, Me many, live—
we cannot, will not, take this to the grave.

For MK

My Husband's Hands

scarred and sturdy
contemplate the possibilities
of sampaguita, bougainvillea.
Crescent moon nails fill
with dirt and sand.
Setting rocks around
mounds of earth,
he picks the first pepper,
its skin sturdy as the hands
that hold it.
He tells me in a voice
firm as rocks set in soil:
What we love, we can hold.
I bend down low,
take a shell white petal in my hand,
and smell the sampaguita.

For My Husband, on the Aging of His Mother

When did you two become friends?
Is that what happens eventually
to sons who come to know
a mother when the care changes hands—
from the first soft, pink palm
to the sturdy gripped and chapped one,
helping her from bed to breakfast and then back again,
every day the same rotation of pills and pillows
then seeking a moment when joy can enter,
like a stray cat looking for a lap to purr away the day,
as if there were nothing better to do?

Darnella's Duty

Darnella Frazier is the young woman who filmed the murder of George Floyd on May 25, 2020

How does it feel to be 17,
and just want to hold your life in your
glistening palm, go to the corner
and buy a sparkling water to quench
a parched mouth that longs to sing?

How does it feel to witness
a purpose too cruel
for all your 17 rotations
around a sun you only want to bask in?

How does it feel to beg a name,
witness a life breaking,
while your opened eyes
see loss and corruption corralled
to the borderless sky?

And, how does the humid wind feel
as you watch it carry one man's life
to a crevice where only the wind can go?

Anniversary

I don't know a love that does not chip away
at the day to day of what couples us.
Every act of creation, also an act of destruction,
and memory is history's great reviser.

The years pass, the regrets mount,
but so does the shared light
we both enjoy at sunset,
the song of the brown thrasher
hidden in our magnolia tree.

We strain to catch a glimpse before it flies—
this memory implanted on its wingspread
soaring away with a piece of what's been shared.

Jenga

Jenga is derived from *kujenga*, a Swahili word which means *to build*. It is also the name of game that removes blocks from a tower.

The space between us,
the years of building our tower—
in this game, wooden blocks
make for an unstable structure—
the goal, to keep
all that's been built upright,
so that what is taken away
does not tumble.
After all this time
we take our turns
and sometimes win
in this game of build and balance.

Sleeping Without My Son

On those nights,
the wind in from Siberia
and trampling across loose roof tiles
he stowed himself between the two of us,
stretching the weave
of a threadbare winter comforter.

His lithe six- year- old body
slithered between us chilling our dreams.
When asked why he came every night
into our chorus of snores,
he mused that we didn't sleep alone,
why should he?

Tonight, reassured that he sleeps with another,
I doze in the cacophony of aged airways
that will never lull me the way a child
desiring not to sleep alone came like a whisper
determined not to be drowned out by the wind.

In That Moment

So entangled in our lives
we just know, when we witness wonder—
times simple as standing
behind a child in the grocery
who cajoles her mother
to allow a lollipop
and flashes a victorious smile.

Our eyes hook
upon what each is thinking—
three decades ago, we too delivered
our child into the world.

We forget the wonder
until the tumult of memory
pulls us apart then pushes us together,
locking us in the twine and twig
that tugs at our history and never breaks.

ACKNOWLEDGMENTS

The poet is grateful to the following magazines for publishing the following poems:

Literary North: Asunción

Silver Birch Press: Wonder and Words

Exquisite Pandemic: The Wind Speaks

Conestoga Zen: Infinite Tenderness, and The Weight of Silence

The New Voices News: Darnella's Duty

Persimmon Tree and Awakenings: Survivors

Raven's Perch: What's Sent Our Way, By Invitation Only, Partaking, Khartoum to Karachi

Indiana Voice Journal: Hands, Debussy at Dusk, Starfish and Sons, A Basket Set By the Shore

Osho Magazine: Morocco in a Moment, The Weight of Silence, Kansha Sai, By Invitation Only, Hands

Poetry Breakfast: Silk Kimono Jacket, Self Portrait, For the Broken

Conche.s Magazine: By Invitation Only, The Weight of Silence

50 Word Stories: Lessons in Electricity, To Do In Quarantine

Poetry Bay: Wabi Sabi

iO Literary Magazine: Apples and Oranges

Roanoke Review: 50 Year Anthology: Infinite Tenderness

Awakenings Art Exhibit on Survivors of Sexual Violence: Survivors: After Stories of Many

Elevation Review's Poetry Podcast LKMNDS featuring Not Drowning, But Waving, Darnella's Duty

Best of the Net Nomination 2019: Self Portrait

I am so appreciative of the time that first readers took with initial drafts of many of these poems, gratitude to Michelle Noullet, Steven DeBonis, Irene Zabytko, and Leslie Ullman.

Laurie Kuntz is an award-winning poet and film producer. She taught creative writing and poetry in Japan, Thailand and the Philippines. Many of her poetic themes are a result of her working with Southeast Asian refugees for over a decade after the Vietnam War years. She has published one poetry collection (*Somewhere in the Telling*, Mellen Press) and two chapbooks (*Simple Gestures*, Texas Review Press and *Women at the Onsen*, Blue Light Press), as well as an ESL reader (*The New Arrival*, Books 1 & 2, Prentice Hall Publishers). Her poetry has been nominated for a Pushcart Prize and The Best of the Net. Her chapbook, *Simple Gestures*, won the Texas Review Poetry Chapbook Contest. She was editor in chief of *Blue Muse Magazine* and a guest editor of *Hunger Mountain Magazine*. She was listed in Glimmer Train's Top 25 Poets. She was twice a finalist in The Nation\Discovery Contest.

Her poetry has been published in *The Bloomsbury Review, The MacGuffin, The Louisville Review, The Charlotte Poetry Review, The Roanoke Review, The Southern Review, The Eleventh Muse, Poetry Miscellany, The New Virginia Review, Crosscurrents, The South Florida Review, The Contemporary Review* and other magazines.

She is a researcher for the upcoming film, *Strangers to Peace*, a documentary on the peace process and reintegration of guerrilla soldiers in Colombia. She produced the short film *Do Tell* a documentary on the repeal of the Don't Ask, Don't Tell Law. She is the executive producer of an Emmy winning short narrative film, *Posthumous*. She holds an MFA in Writing from Vermont College. Recently retired, she lives in an endless summer state of mind. Her website is: https://lauriekuntz.myportfolio.com/home-1

www.ingramcontent.com/pod-product-compliance
Lightning Source LLC
Chambersburg PA
CBHW021151090426
42740CB00008B/1039